Communion

Nahshon Cook

Communion

Copyright © 2018 by Nahshon Cook

All rights reserved. No part of this book may be reproduced or transmitted in any form or by any means without written permission of the author.

Cover art: "Chalice," from the Candela Series by T.M. Davy

Library of Congress Control Number: 2018940469

ISBN: 978-0-9600931-7-5

Published by Shabda Press
Pasadena, CA 91107
www.shabdapress.com

Contents

After Watching Philando Castille Die on Facebook Live 1
Love: 1. 2
Self-Portrait as Joe. 3
Self-Portrait as K.C. 5
Meditation. 6
From a Telephone Conversation with My Mother: 1 8
Work Poem: 1 9
Self-Portrait as B.:1 11
Sex 12
While We Were Lying Awake in Bed Early This Morning 13
Listening to an Old Man Vent In the Lobby At Discount Tire
    This Morning 14
This Morning 15
From Lenny's Memorial Service. 17
Requiem 19
A Poem About B. 21
Self-Portrait as The Buddha 22
Evening News. 23
Evening News Interview with Neighbor X: Day 1 24
Today. 26
A Lament 28
From the Sermon Preached at Her Funeral 30
Her Burial. 32
A Poem for the Man Who Murdered My Cousin Last September . . . 34
Trying to Go to Sleep 35
At A Stop Sign 36
Work Poem: 2 38
In Protest of Darren Wilson's Being Found Not Guilty: Civic
    Center Park. Denver, CO. 39
Body 41

Notes from Pine Ridge (1): A Young Lakota Man 43
A Mushroom. 44
Eric Garner 46
A Story B. Told Me About When He Was in College. 48
Notes from A Dream 49
Wedding Poem 50
A Story My Mom Told Me. 53
Driving 55
A Poem About War 57
In America 58
Work Poem: 3 59
At Three O'clock This Morning 60
Today, April 17, 2015, 10:25 A.M. 61
The Old Lady Sitting Next to Me on the Plane Ride back to Denver: 2 . . . 63
This Morning's Prayer. 65
Race for The Cure 66
The Police 68
A Voicemail from Kit After Not Hearing from Her for Eight Months . . . 69
With Kit at Denver Health (2) 70
With Kit at Denver Health (3) 72
Elephant 74
Waiting for My Pancakes 75
Just Listening to Kit Talk 77
Kit Goes to Hospice 78
Visiting Kit in Hospice: 1 80
Talking to the Hospice Chaplain on the Phone 82
Visiting Kit in Hospice: 2 83
Corpus Christi 84
Porn. 85
Imagine 87
Children of God: 1 88
Children of God: 2 90
I Asked Him to Marry Me 91
Nova 93
Sergio: 1. 95

Another Poem About B.	97
Memories of Thailand: 3	99
Self-Portrait as Har	100
After Yoga This Morning	102
Self-Portrait as Janice	103
Our First Kiss	105
in the summer between the third and fourth grade	106
A Rough Patch: 1	107
Communion	109
Self-Portrait as My Sister: 1	110
From A Letter	112
From A Telephone Conversation with My Mother: 2	113
Telephone	114
Love: 2	115
Transcendence	116
Sergio: 2	117
Trying To Pay Bills	118
Going to Bed	119
Something New and Gentle	120
Self-Portrait as My Sister: 2	121
On Kit's First Birthday Since Her Death	123
Pregnancy	125
Buddhahood	126

After Watching Philando Castille Die on Facebook Live

if by chance
a cop pulls me over

and kills me
for no reason

please know
i don't have a gun

i believe
with all my heart

they've outlived
their usefulness

they don't protect
anyone from anyone

they hurt
everyone

also know
i'm not afraid to die

just like
i'm not afraid to live

i'm thankful for this life
it's my last one

i don't ever want
to come back here again

Love: 1

she said
love is

a lot like
a sparrow

if it comes
let it land

but be prepared
to let it go

Self-Portrait as Joe

I asked Joe
How he knew

Robert was the one
He wanted to be with

Well, Joe said,
It took a while

For our slow
Kind of quiet

At-home-ness
To develop

We've been together
Thirteen years

And married
One year today

To tell the truth
I don't think

It's so much
A discovery

As a commitment
To talk and to listen

Honestly
To one another

That's how we
Make us work

But if there was
A moment

It was when
I first saw

How lovingly
He treated my father

Self-Portrait as K.C.

For my internship
I mentor an eleven-year-old

Asperger's kiddo
At Denver Mental Health

Who's being adopted
By a gay couple in D.C.

He'll be going out to visit them
For a week in a few days

Yesterday
I was talking to him

About the fight
For civil rights

Going back to slavery
And voting rights for Blacks

Then women's rights
Then Native Americans

Then gay rights
And-on and-on

When I finished
He looked at me and said

I thought you were only supposed
To make a mistake once

Meditation

I sat facing the window
on my meditation pillow

with legs folded in pretzel pose
contemplating the possibility

of being alive beginning to mean
happiness is found in learning

to navigate pain in order
to move through it then let it go

when the ticking seconds' hand
of the pink analog clock

hanging on the wall behind me
began guiding my thoughts

to the space in my heart
where I go to be in love

I closed my eyes
and saw a small splotch of blue light

when I focused on it
my mind silenced itself

that's when I began feeling
a pulsing sensation

on the back of my head
like someone was knocking on my cranium

the more I focused on the light
the stronger the pulsing got

then I felt a pop
like a little explosion

and there was a sudden rush of energy
that oozed through me like a flood

my body was tingling
my hands felt like fire

From a Telephone Conversation with My Mother: 1

People
—in the end,

just like
in the beginning—

are people.
And people

will break
your heart.

Go into all
your relationships

knowing this
and you'll be okay.

Work Poem: 1

1)
Then he told me
how he and his husband

brought their seven-year-old
to the hospital

because she'd had
sixty seizures

in five hours. He said
The neurologists

ran a bunch
of inconclusive tests

and told us
they didn't know

what was wrong
with her brain. He said

I envy the family
with the kid with cancer. He said,

At least they have an answer.
All we want to know, he said,

is if we should be planning
for college or hospice.

2)
That evening
I went to La Fogata

for dinner. I ordered
three cheese enchiladas

with a side of rice
and beans, no onion.

A live mariachi band played
beautiful Mexican music while I ate.

Self-Portrait as B.:1

I told
my uncle

about me
and you.

He said
as long as

I'm happy.
I told

my cousin, too.
He said

we have to go
on a hike

sometime.
My uncle

told me
I might meet

a little resistance
from the older

people and
kinda looked

in my grandma's
direction.

Sex

i used to think
if we had

great sex
he'd love me more

and wouldn't leave
i've since learned

that's not how
to make love stay

While We Were Lying Awake in Bed Early This Morning

he said: what is
something
you don't know?

i said: how to be
a better boyfriend to you.
when I talked
to my mom about it,

she said:
we don't know
what we don't know.

she said:
but be honest
and stay open
to learn.

he said: your mom
gives good advice.

i said: yes she does.

Listening to an Old Man Vent In the Lobby At Discount Tire This Morning

I'm not doing bad
For an old geezer

Life now
Is just a matter of pain

And what doctor
You go to to cure it

Retirement isn't all
It's cut out to be

I tell you kid
Never get old

I'm not saying
It's all bad

I had cancer
And I think it's gone away

But I'm not as strong
As I was—my body

I used to be able
To work on my cars

But now I can't
Even lift a tire

I tell you kid
Stay young forever

This Morning

This morning
after his alarm went off
and he awoke
and got out of bed
to use the bathroom
then take a shower
I sat up
and contemplated
the depression
he left in the sheets
for a few minutes
then grabbed my notebook and pen
off the nightstand
and started writing about
the memorial candles
for his brother and father
on either side
of the steel effigy of Jesus
hanging on a bronze cross
on the very top of his bookshelf

He was standing
at the sink
with a blue towel
wrapped around his waist
brushing his teeth
in front of the mirror
when I began wishing
his palms were resting
on the back of my head

with finger tips
messaging my scalp
while I sucked his dick
but we were both
pressed for time
he had class at nine-thirty
and I had to get across town
for my friend, Lenny's,
memorial service
at the pavilion
in Cheesman Park by ten

From Lenny's Memorial Service

I sat back
in my black metal
fold-out chair
with right leg
crossed over left
and hands interlaced
into a loosely balled fist
resting on my lap
while I listened
to Lenny's daughter
retell a story
her dad shared with her
the day before he died
about how a street guy
came up to him
and asked if he
had anything for a bum.
She said: *My father said,*
'I walked right up to the guy
and told him:
You're not a bum,
you're a man of God.'
She was dressed
in a black sleeveless blouse,
a matching pair
of silk pants with huge
pink floral prints,
and black leather shoes.

And was standing
in front of a rectangular table
covered in cloth,
almost like an altar.
It was holding glass vases
full of freshly cut flowers
and photograph portraits
of her, now, dearly departed darling.
The most beautiful thing
to me about my father,
she continued, was that
he only spoke in words
that were obvious to the heart.
His love was a safe place
for any of us to be
completely where we were at
without judgement
or criticism or blame
because he knew
people belong to each other
like family, she said.
His love was home.

Requiem

Those two young men
You could call them boys
Strung him up
To a wooden fence
On the side of the road
And beat him to a bloody abstraction
Nine days later
October 16 1998
Softly falling snowflowers fell
On a small congregation
Of crucifying Christians
Who stood across the street
From the red-brick Episcopal church
On the corner
Of South Wolcott and East 7th
And protested his memorial service
With little black leather-bound Bibles
And lewd signs
And filthy mouths shouting
God's supposed hate for gays
One of the most beautiful things
I've ever seen is the sun
Shinning its light into a world
Where wars are fought
To try'n keep people
From being who they are
And even though sometimes
It feels like everything I've done

Up till now has been wrong
I still think fighting over religion is stupid
It's like calling someone Jean
Whose name is George
And expecting them to answer
And the more I pray and the more I live
The more I see that truly being
A human being means love
And love means helping someone else
Find their own way
Whether this is true or not
I don't know
But sometimes
We have to deceive ourselves
To stay alive and keep going

A Poem About B.

He's begun finding
out about my

childhood and all
my past and all

my pain and all
my mistakes and all

my weirdness and
my strange ways

of being in the world
and has decided

it's worth his time
to still be there

like the sunrise
every morning

Self-Portrait as The Buddha

I've realized
that when you've grown

tired of being
what you're not

and start celebrating
who you are

you begin
to understand

that fighting
for freedom

is not the purpose
of this journey

but rather
it is seeing

that you
are already free

Evening News

I just
received word

my cousin
was murdered

in Memphis
earlier today

trying to protect
her sister

from her sister's
boyfriend.

Two guns
were found in the house.

And except for
those of us

who knew
and love her

she's nothing more
than evening news.

Evening News Interview with Neighbor X: Day 1

Actually
I was in the shower

When I heard
Loud beats at the door

It was the young lady
Who lives

Right over here
Across the street

Askin' if she
Could use the phone

To call 911
So they could send

An ambulance
Because the guy

Over there
Shot her sister

She said *like*
Six-or-seven times

This ain't nothin' new
It's sad

And there's no way
To wrap your mind around it

But this ain't nothin' new
I've seen this before

Today

1)
my aunt and
uncle went

to identify her body
at the funeral home

they said
he shot her

in the leg
in the stomach

in the arm
and the right brow

and that her head
is so swollen

she's not even
recognizable

2)
at her vigil
there was a man

in a black t-shirt
who said

if you got brothers
cousins uncles

and you know
they are mistreating

women
you need to get

to your brother
today

and tell them
it's wrong

A Lament

My heart
breaks
a little more
each time
I try'n imagine
how it happened:
that she has
left her body
behind
so soon
to a life
of its own,
with us,
and gone on
to something
we know
nothing about
except
that it's
very different.
I wonder,
what did God
have in mind?
When informed
he'd been arrested
on charges
of attempted
first degree murder,

Neighbor Y
told reporters:
None of us
knows
what we'd do
if a gun
was cocked to our head
he had scratches
on his face
like
a wild animal
had gone off
on him.
If he did
try to do
to his girlfriend
like he did
to her sister,
I'm sure
it was in
self-defense.

From the Sermon Preached at Her Funeral

in his sermon
the preacher said
God is good
even in the midst
of all our grief
and all our pain
he said
God is still God
and God is still
on the throne
he said
we are not here
because she died
he said
we are here
because she lived
he said
she was good people
he said
we can praise God
for her life
he said
let us celebrate
that she's up there
with Big Mama
havin' a time

he said
she's no longer
in this cruel world
he said
she's resting
in Jesus' arms

Her Burial

it'd been decided
her final resting place
would be next to
our great grandmother
and was prepared
with a cement vault
that lay waiting patiently
to receive her
beautifully held body
eight of us carried her
from the hearse
to a forest green hilltop tent
stretched out over
a skirted stainless-steel rectangle
perfectly picture-framing
the heavy-heartedness
she was slowly lowered into
once we'd all said
our final goodbyes
my father and I
stayed to watch
the undertaker supervise
his gravediggers
in covering her casket
first with the vault's lid
then a dump truck bed
full of wet heavy earth
he shook hands with us both

and apologized
for our unfortunate loss
before explaining
how they'd allow the dirt
to settle during winter
then cover her plot
with sod in spring

A Poem for the Man Who Murdered My Cousin Last September

I want to hate you
but I don't

if I did
you'd win

and since the only thing
I know how to do

without a doubt
is believe in God

you sir
are forgiven

Trying to Go to Sleep

This morning
    after getting home from work
    I laid down to go to sleep
    but when I closed my eyes
    I saw my cousin lying dead
    in the crime scene photo
she was on her back next to a wall
she was dressed in all black
her eyelids were half closed
her pupils were glassy and blank
her left palm was on her stomach
her right palm was on the floor
    facing up with half-clinched fingers
there was a small tunnel drilled
    in her forehead from a bullet
her braids sprawled out on the carpet
    from her scalp like cast divination sticks
a little housefly was resting
    on the tip of her nose

At A Stop Sign

I was stopping
at a stop sign
on my way home
from work last night
when I flipped through
the radio stations
to 1390 AM
and caught the tail end
of a speech
recorded at a rally
in Washington
by a woman
who said: *Innocent people*
are being shot down
like animals.
She said: *Parents*
have to go home
to empty rooms
because their children's lives
are being taken away
by people
who shouldn't have guns
in the first place.
She said: Gun enthusiasts
keep talking about
their Second
Amendment Right.

*But, what about
people's right to live?
She said: This
is genocide
in America.*
When the time
for commercials returned,
I took a few deep breaths
pressed the CD button
on the stereo faceplate
and put Aretha Franklin's
1972 recording
 of Amazing Grace
on repeat.

Work Poem: 2

1)
At the beginning of Check-In Group, I had the kids say what'd brought them to the hospital. When this particular young lady's turn came around, she said: *A little orange bottle full of white sleeping pills.*

2)
As she continued to answer the rest of my questions about how her family visit went at supper-time and how her treatment work was coming along, I—for some reason—was reminded of my neighbor Cindy's older sister, who'd attempted suicide—when they were teenagers—by sitting, bent over the edge of her desk chair, with their father's shotgun clamped between her knees, its barrel aimed at her heart.

When Cindy's sister pulled the trigger, the kickback caused the gun's barrel to shift. The shot blew Cindy's sister's left arm clean off—and took her eyesight away. I imagine blood and tissue and bone spattering all over the walls and ceiling of Cindy's sister's bedroom like colors in Jackson Pollack's painting *No. 8.*

3)
Their mother found Cindy's sister still alive and called the ambulance. The doctors at the hospital saved Cindy's sister's life.

4)
My last question to the young lady, before we moved on to the next person in the group, was, "What words of wisdom do you have for the rest of us?" She said: *Everyone deserves a lifetime,* she said. *And I know there's a world outside of here for me to find a place in,* she said. *And I will.*

In Protest of Darren Wilson's Being Found Not Guilty: Civic Center Park. Denver, CO.

When I arrived
A middle-aged

Humpty-Dumpty
Shaped woman

With hair as short as ants
Was telling protestors

How those cops
In Ferguson

Wanted them to riot.
She said, *They want*

To beat you
With their sticks

And take you to jail
Because the 'Establishment'

Has just thumbed
It's nose at you

And has told you,
Once again,

That you
Don't matter.

Don't do it,
She said.

Stay calm.
Walk softly.

Pray loudly.
Go home.

Body

our relationship
has been a long one

it began during the summer
between my fifth

and sixth grade years
of middle school

when I started wearing
big winter sweaters

to hide the fact
that I couldn't button

my jeans anymore
since then

life has been
one lesson

after another
in the rules

of being a big girl
tucking herself

in undergarments
to make outfits acceptable

just this morning
while getting dressed

I stood in front of the mirror
with my belly in my hands and shook it

when I was younger
I would fantasize about

taking a pair of scissors
and cutting it off

Notes from Pine Ridge (1): A Young Lakota Man

We're poor, he said,
but we are free.

Ours isn't the illusion of freedom;
our freedom is reality.

Earlier that evening
I'd offered him a coat.

Naw, brotha, he said,
I have buffalo skin.

When I offered again
more time had passed,

it was a little colder.
The wind had begun to grow.

He paused for a few seconds
and said, *Sure.*

Thanks, man.
This coat is nice.

Then he stuck his hand
in his pants pocket

and handed me a bullet.
Here, he said, we believe in tradin'.

A Mushroom

1)
I was laying on my back on the couch, resting my head on B.'s lap, while he softly ran his index finger down the middle of my face. When he got to my chin, he blinked a few times and told me my bottom lip looked like a mushroom sticking out from the side of a tree. We kissed.

Then I shared with him the story about the time I was at *H&R Block*, sitting across the desk from the accountant doing my taxes, when a lady, who'd locked her keys in her car, began talking to the receptionist while she waited for her friend to bring a hanger.

After offering the lady a cup of coffee, the receptionist shared a story about how it once took him an hour to find his car because he'd forgotten where he'd parked. *"I do silly things like that when I'm in love,"* he said. When the lady denied the possibility of there being anyone in her world for whom she would leave the past behind and start anew, the receptionist said, *"The person in love is usually the last one to know."*

2)
Later that evening, while B. lay in bed sleeping, I was back downstairs in the dining room working on a poem about being in Estes Park and sitting on the knotty-pine cabin porch in the shadow of a huge shade tree while listening to Ron share what it was like for him to be a young gay man in the early-eighties stage in the age of AIDS.

3)

Morning came and I was awakened from a dream by a bright beam of white light streaming through the kitchen window like a revelation. In the dream, I was a rocking chair with super powers: every time you sat in it it took you to the moon and gave you a milk shake.

Before I got up to go to the bathroom, I took a deep breath, opened my eyes, thanked God for the day, then said a prayer for the kid at work who—yesterday afternoon during "Room Time"—explained to me the picture he'd made earlier in Art Therapy Group. He said: *This fan on the table is the past. This vase has cracks in it because the fan keeps blowing the vase off the table. I'm the vase. This is a jar of glue I've used to piece the vase together. I'm here because I ran out of glue. Cocaine is the hammer I used to try'n smash the vase to bits.*

Eric Garner

We were peacefully protesting
in the intersection
of Colfax Avenue
and Speer Boulevard,
when a white Honda Sedan
sped through the police barricade
and began rolling toward us.
As the car neared
a small crowd
of loud white voices rang out
from one of the windows
of the tall red brick
apartment building
opposite Auraria campus,
egging the driver on
to run us over.

On the drive home
I listened to a reporter on BBC
describe that days'
Bramhall's cartoon
for December 2014.
He said: *She's laying
blind-folded on a sidewalk
next to the sewer
with scales flung back
overhead and sword
dropped down by her side.*

Above her body, the words:
"I can't breathe"
are written in quote bubbles.
The title of the piece is:
'Justice System and Eric Garner.'

A Story B. Told Me About When He Was in College

we were alone
and had started kissing
my heart was pounding
I was sweating
we'd gone from zero-to-sixty
in like two seconds
next thing I know
his dick's in my mouth
I asked him to stop
he said But you want it
I don't remember
how many times
I asked him to stop
but at one point
he had me pinned to the bed
he was holding me down
by the shoulders
with his hands
and because he was bigger than I was
I wasn't able to push him off
even when I tried
and I tried really hard
until I just kinda gave up

Notes from A Dream

a little girl
dressed

in black
single-button shoes

a blue lace-collared dress
and a wide

straw sun hat
brim-banded

with flowers
and butterflies

is eating
one of the red heart-

shaped apples
she'd picked

from an old tree
planted

a very long
long time ago

by someone
who wanted love

to keep
growing

Wedding Poem

1)
he handed her
a big box

with nine smaller boxes
each inside the other

all wrapped
in soft gold gift paper

the last of which
held a neatly folded

hand-written note
she'd read

while he walked across
the living room floor

to a shelf on the wall
and pulled out

a small midnight blue
rectangular case

from behind
a red wooden mask

they'd bought
on their last trip to Mexico

then he got down on one knee
opened the lid

asked her *Please marry me*
she smiled and said *Of course*

nine months ago
on Christmas Day

2)
Anna and Bryson
you're both already

further along than I
finding and living in love

with someone who
loves you for you

and together learning
to help love stay

so there's not much
I can say about

making you-all's
closeness last

but I do know
that our lives

are the memory
of moments

that can never
be lived again

it is my prayer
that when the end

of this road nears
as it inevitably will

and assisted living
becomes hospice

that you can still
hold hands and look

into each other eyes
and realize that happiness

is knowing you'd do it
all again if you could

A Story My Mom Told Me

I was in the front yard
raking the lawn

when she came over
and said, "I've been drinkin'.

"and I know we dun
talked for years,

"but this mother-fucker
try'n to make me
lose my kids.

"If my kids come
knockin' on your door,
askin' you
to call the police.

"Please," she said,
"call the police."

I took a deep breath
then told her
to get a restraining order.

She looked sad and said,
"I may have to."

Look at what's at stake,

I said:

*If you're havin'
a hard time choosing
between your man
and your kids,
choose your kids.*

I said:

They need you.

Driving

Yesterday afternoon,
on my way to the supermarket,
I heard a blurb on the radio
for a news report about religion
being used as a form of torture
by American soldiers
on Gitmo Prison Muslims,
in which a retired Episcopal Priest,
protesting in front of the White House,
with a sign, expressed his astonishment
over how any true believer
in Jesus Christ—Who, the priest said,
was also tortured and killed by the State—
could try'n justify the torture
of anyone else.

When the blurb was over
I turned the radio off.
I was driving west down Colfax Avenue
and had turned right on Airport Boulevard
then left onto Gun Club
where I saw a bald eagle
standing in the middle of a prairie dog field
like a snow-capped mountain.
I turned right on to Hampden.
I took Hampden to Pichadilly.

At Pichadilly, I turned left at the light,
then drove a little ways—past the high school
and the middle school and the fire station—
before turning right
into the supermarket parking lot,
where I found a space to park my car.
Then I went inside with the intention
of buying ginger snaps,
to eat with my oatmeal for breakfast,
but they were all out.

A Poem About War

I imagine her taking another sip of tea, turning the page in her notebook and beginning to share a poem she said she'd begun working on recently about her time in the Army as a convoy medic and how one day while driving down Fourteenth of July Street, in Baghdad, one of her comrades shot up a civilian car, from a Humvee with a fifty-caliber machine gun, for passing too closely, *Because,* she said, *the world is a battlefield full of dirty wars were the only thing that matters is me and the ones I'm with: everyone else be damned,— right?*

I post my elbows on the table, lower my chin between my palms, close my eyes and turn my whole body into an ear listening to her read about how a young Arab man got out of the car covered in blood, with four bullet wounds to the chest, and collapsed in the street before beginning to float in-and-out of consciousness like things in a dark room lit by a flickering light bulb. She said, *When I finally got to him, he'd already stopped breathing,* she said, *so I took my left hand and lifted his chin, and put my right hand on the back of his head to position it for CPR only to find I was palming his brain.* She said, *There was nothing I could do.* She said, *You can't stop bleeding from the head like that.*

In America

when I walked into
the feed store

to buy Nova more oats
and stall shavings

the old man was behind
the counter watching

live news coverage
of the attacks in Paris

he asked
how I was doing

I said *The world*
he said *Is crazy*

after he gave me
my receipt

I wished him
a beautiful day

he said *I feel
thankful and*

*very blessed we live
where we live*

Work Poem: 3

yes, we're talking about attempting suicide
    by ingesting fifteen pills of Antabuse
    and washing it down
    with a glass of scotch

yes, we're talking about waking up in the morning
    and because you don't have booze
    drinking shaving lotion
    just to get alcohol out of it

yes, we're talking about going into convulsions
    and going into seizures
    and going into black outs
    that you almost never came out of

yes, we're talking about you deciding
    whether or not it's worth it for you to live

but, what's the reason
    we're talking about these things

At Three O'Clock This Morning

five cop cars
a fire truck

and an ambulance
just left

my neighbor's house
two doors down

it was crazy
this big black bald guy

was yelling
loud as hell

that she
(my neighbor)

was a fake bitch
the police had him

handcuffed
in the front yard

sounded like maybe
he was a new boyfriend

Today, April 17, 2015, 10:25 A.M.

I was driving East
on Smith Road
toward Airport Boulevard,
thinking about
what love is
and where it's found
when I saw a white
Pontiac Grand Am
crashed into a light pole
on the side of the road,
and a young man
laying on the grass
in the snow.
I pulled over
and got out of my car
to see how I could help.
There was already a person
covering the young man
with an olive-green blanket.
Another person
in an orange
Home Depot apron
said, He's going into shock.
An ambulance is on the way.
When I knelt down
and said, Hello,
the young man

reached his left hand out
trying to give me
his cell phone.
When I asked his name
he opened his eyes
and said, Daniel.

The Old Lady Sitting Next to Me on the Plane Ride back to Denver: 2

I usually have a dictionary
when I do my crossword puzzles

because I don't know
what all the words mean.

But, it's too hard to bring
a dictionary on the plane.

They say anything you can do
to use your mind:

I have two sisters
who have Alzheimer's.

I'm fighting back as hard as I can.
Did I tell you that already?

You know, my hips are bad.
I've gotten the right hip replaced.

The doctors say I need
a new left one, too.

I'm fighting getting surgery
even though

I have a harder time
walking than before.

Did I already tell you
this is my last time

getting on a plane?
I told my kids

if they want to see me after this trip
they have to come to Granite Falls.

There's a lot of granite
in Granite Falls,

and waterfalls and a river,
and we kinda have a valley.

This Morning's Prayer

Last night
I watched

The dash-cam police video
Marking

The beginning
Of Sandra Bland's end

This morning
Before walking out

The front door
To leave the house

And go to work
I closed my eyes

And prayed
This prayer

Don't be afraid
All they can take

Is your body
It's already dust

Amen

Race for The Cure

After I told my mom
how being with her
for my first time
at Race for the Cure
among so many people
in pink, holding posters
in memory of loved ones
breast cancer had cut down
reminded me of the time
I visited an old temple in Nepal
whose walls were tattooed
in murals of fierce-looking gods
with glaring eyes and
gritted teeth and
sharp knives and
long swords. And
how hard getting past
the implied scariness
of it all was, at first.
But how, once I'd entered
the silence of the sanctuary,
my heart was able
to find peace,
with itself,
again.

My mom
looked at me
and said: *Yes, it just*
goes to show
how you have to
keep moving forward
on so many levels.

The Police

I was driving
Down the street

Considering
How scary a time

It is right now
In the country

Bland being
Pulled over

For not using
Her turn signal

Dubose's
License plate

It makes me wonder
If the police

Pull me over
Should I stop

It just might
Go wrong

A Voicemail from Kit After Not Hearing from Her for Eight Months

The pressure
From the tumor

In my intestines
Created a third hole

Between my rectum
And vagina

I started leaking
My plumbing's fucked up

I'm here in the E.R
At Denver Health

I just wanted someone
To know where I am

With Kit at Denver Health (2)

I told them
to hold off

on the surgery
till Monday

they want to
re-route

my intestines
to a bag

so I can
heal

as far as
the cancer

my liver's
involved

I told them
I didn't want

aggressive
treatment

the oncologist
agrees

chemo's not
the way to go

What does
the oncologist

suggest
I asked

she said
Hospice

With Kit at Denver Health (3)

If I wake up
I'm thankful

to be able
to make

the most
of the day

some days
I'm thankful

for the sun
other days

I'm thankful
for the rain

this cancer
is scary

but no more scary
than getting shot at

or being
homeless

or a lot of
other stuff

I've lived
through

I've learned
when you're

not afraid
of losing

you always
always win

no matter
what happens

Elephant

Last night
one of my co-workers

told me about
how her toddler

got out of the bathtub
before his bedtime on Tuesday

touched his penis
and said *Elephant*

after I nearly died
laughing myself to tears

she said
he is two years old

there are a few words
he knows well

Elephant
is one of them

Waiting for My Pancakes

1)
This morning
the drive between work

and Village Inn
was spent listening

to a news story on NPR about
live house band Blues concerts

being played
every Sunday for forty years

in the garage of an old man
in South Central L.A.

2)
Waiting for my pancakes
I contemplate Kit

in the hospital
with terminal cancer

and our visit yesterday
during brunch

She told me she feels
rested enough

to believe
in miracles again

then read me
her new poem about God

It says

*We look
to the clouds*

*instead of listen
to our hearts*

Just Listening to Kit Talk

last night
in the silence

I told God
if I have

more work
to do

I'm willing
and to please

give me
more time

but if it's time
I'm willing

to be
welcomed home

either way
I'm ready

to be done
sitting

in this
hospital bed

Kit Goes to Hospice

This afternoon
I received a call

From a social worker
Informing me

Kit had entered the home
For the last part of her life

And that they'd need a copy
Of the Power of Attorney

And that I could drop it off
Next time I went to see her

They said she said
It was okay to contact you

It is I said then asked
Where is she at exactly

They wouldn't tell me
The name of the place

Well I said *it's nice to know*
She's still alive

I've called her almost every day
For the past three months

And have left a message
When her voicemail wasn't full

And today I hear from her
Through you about this

That's pretty fucked up I think
Don't you

Do me a favor will you please
Tell her to call me herself

Visiting Kit in Hospice: 1

she's in this room
with three tan walls

and a big window
and a twin bed

where she lay
with limp head

and blue-socked feet
sticking out from under the covers

there's no fat on her
patiently dying face

with its dark bulging eyes
and pulled back wrinkly lips

and the big black
cavity growing

in the chipped off tip
of her top left front tooth

she looks tired
and shrunken

and frail and
so very beautiful

before I get up to leave
I tell her I love you pretty lady

she blows me a kiss then says
I love you too friend

Talking to the Hospice Chaplain on the Phone

after he explained the process
to get a voucher

from The Department of Human Services
I told him she likely didn't have a bank account

and also that she was homeless
well, he said, in that case

if you don't want
to get involved

and she doesn't have any money
the State will take over her case

and they'll cremate her
and dump her ashes

in the county's mass grave
for unclaimed people

Visiting Kit in Hospice: 2

I sat by her bedside
holding her hand

tears falling
from my eyes

as she lay sleeping
the pain of death away

I told her
how thankful I am

we're friends
and how sorry I am

I couldn't do more
to help her

*I'm used to moving
mountains*

*for you I said
but now*

*all I can do
is sit here*

*and hold your hand
and cry*

Corpus Christi

I was sitting in the living room
On the love seat watching

My kitten Butterfly sleep
In front of blue-hearted flames

Crackling in the fireplace
Above which a beautiful

Bronze bodied Jesus hangs on the wall
With diaphragm and coil pot ribs

Protruding through sunken flesh
Like desert waves

His left leg rests on his right
A single nail attaches his feet

To the thin vertical piece
Of polished pine cross

Sometimes I still believe
In things I know aren't true

Porn

I was at my computer
jerking off

to a very pretty
hairy-legged twink

with a beautiful
sleeve tattooed

on his right arm
of an emerald green-eyed koi fish

swimming around
in a crystal clear pond

with yellow flower blossoms
floating on the surface

he was getting his
back door knocked on

by a shiny Adonis
whose perfect body

I wished I could
identify with in some way

when B. called and asked
what I was up to

I said watching porn
with men in it

B. said
That's hot

Imagine

imagine
going to church

and experiencing
the sky

and the water
and the earth

coming
together

all at once
inside you

while you
sit in a pew

and listen
to the preacher

preach
the beginning

of the beginning
again

that's what
having

an orgasm
is like for me

Children of God: 1

i can honestly say
life is fucked up

i have five kids
i can't provide for

because i'm sick
and can't work

that's the kind of shit
that makes a mother

want to kill herself
and kill her kids

because i don't want
to be a burden

and have to beg
anybody for anything

i'm broke and poor
i want these chains

of bondage off of me
and these kids

they're not slaves
why should they live like this

i don't want my kids
watching me die

i've asked God
to take me away

and give my kids what they need
i know they need me

but if i'm dyin'
they don't need to see that

Children of God: 2

she had a warrant
out for her arrest

for prostitution
and so was taken to jail

after the police were called
because he walked in on her

having sex
with some other dude

so he gathered the kids
and was preparing

to leave the house
when the other dude

walked out the bedroom
with pistol drawn

and began shooting at him
while he was holding

their two-year-old daughter
in his arms

I Asked Him to Marry Me

we were laying
in bed together

my right ear
on his heart

listening
to the calming music

of his softly
breathing body

after a while
I told him

I'd been thinking
about our relationship

and how after a year-
and-a-half of dating

I didn't know
what we were

working towards
anymore

he said: *what about*
you and me

building
a life together

so I asked him
to marry me

that sounds like
a good idea

he said *but*
not right now

Nova

I was sitting
on a huge grey
cement slab
contemplating
the silhouettes
of gnats dancing
around on Nova's coat
like shadow puppets
while he grazed
on green tufts of grass
growing on the side
of Sand Creek
when an old man
came puttering
down the dirt path
on his morning walk.
He saw us, stopped,
said hello, then told me
a story about him
being in college
and riding one of his
neighbor's horses
when the saddle
began sliding off
to the side because
the cinch was too loose;
and how the first thing
he thought to do

was take his feet
out of the stirrups
before he hit the ground
because there was a half-mile
of paved road
back to the barn.
Then he asked
if Nova was
an easy horse to handle.
No, I replied,
he's stubborn,
intelligent,
full of his own ideas,
and is absolutely brilliant.
The old man smiled
and said, *Nova*
sounds a lot like my wife.

Sergio: 1

there's a sixteenth century
German image of a man

lying in bed with his head
resting on a pillow

his body's covered up
to his armpits by a blanket

on one side of him
a crucified Jesus on the wall

being prayed to by
a circle of haloed saints

on the other side
a gang of hell-faced demons

sprouted up from below
Ars Moriendi (The Art of Dying)

the man looks so peaceful
I wondered if that's what

letting go was like
for our cousin Sergio

My sister called this morning
telling me he hadn't survived

being shot in the chest
yesterday afternoon

in the parking lot of Jenny's Market
on 35th and Downing

Another Poem About B.

He turned around
and closed

the blue iron gate
before beginning

to walk through
the tiny village cemetery

on the side
of a mountain

across the valley
from Colorado

when he found the spot
where his brother is buried

he knelt down
in the snow

then placed his palms
on a grey headstone

I watched
from the passenger seat

thinking how
no one

can hold on
to anyone forever

everyone
always goes away

Memories of Thailand: 3

once while I was living in Thailand
one of my very very good friends
got horribly sick while on vacation
with his wife
and infant daughter in Mexico
they lived in Omaha but flew him
to University Hospital in Denver
the doctors didn't know
what was wrong with him
his white blood cell count
was too high to be Leukemia
they did a lumbar puncture
to see if an allergy
had caused his brain to puff up
the doctors told his wife
he's an academically interesting case
in the last picture she posted
he was dressed
in a blue-and-white hospital gown
with a white towel over his eyes
and hands resting on his belly
like a dead person laid in a casket
when I first received the news
I called my mom
hysterical and crying
at three o'clock in morning
Colorado time
she listened to my sadness
then told me to do my yoga
and find my breath. *Right now,*
she said, *he needs your prayers.*

Self-Portrait as Har

Have you ever,
like me,
lost the one you love?

When it feels like
your world
is shattered
and all you have,
all the reasons
for you to wake up each morning,
are gone,
what do you do
when such sadness
devours you?

What could you do?

For me,
I wake up
to my daily routine.
I know that I lost myself.
Waking up is not easy,
it takes time for me
each morning
to become me.

I wash my face,
brush my teeth,
put on my clothes
and have my breakfast.

By the time I'm finished
with my daily ritual
at least I have
half of myself becoming.

It helps me survive.

After Yoga This Morning

I felt my belly move in and out
while I sat cross-legged on my mat

practicing trying to understand myself
a little more deeply with each breath

I once heard it said
or maybe I read it somewhere

that knowing who you are is the only way
to sincerely stay in love with someone else

the serenity-at-the-end-of-the-
yoga-session-buzz wore off

after about ten minutes
trying to visualize

a pink lotus blossom shinning above
a pool of muddy water like the sun

when I opened my eyes
I saw my kitten Butterfly

looking out the living room window
at a squirrel in the front yard

Self-Portrait as Janice

I feel safe
with my husband

if tomorrow
the world ended

if I was with
my husband

and my son
I'd be okay

I've gained weight
since me and my husband met

and I love that our love
has blossomed

beyond physicality
and into the heart

and I love the way
he talks to our son

even when he thinks
I'm not listenin'

and I'm just putterin'
around the house

if somethin' ever happened
we agreed

not to bad-mouth each other
in front of our son

because we have to
prepare him to be a man

in a world that's getting harder
to be in by the day

Our First Kiss

He caressed
my cheekbone

with his fingertips,
before tilting his head

slightly to the right,
and gently—very gently—

touching his soft,
pink lips to mine.

Then he pulled away
and held

the back of my head
in his palms

and looked into my eyes,
and I looked into his

and said: *Good night,
and thank you*

for a wonderful evening
He smiled and said,

"The pleasure was all mine.
Thank you, too."

in the summer between the third and fourth grade

a big black sedan
zoomed off
down 16th Street
towards Kingston
then sped through the stop sign
and skid around the corner
up towards E. Colfax
I looked in the direction
of the fired shots
and saw the body of a guy
lying face down
on the side walk
across the street
from a milk-white stucco
five story apartment building
with brown rectangular framed
cheaply draped windows
blood was gushing
from the back of his head

A Rough Patch: 1

This afternoon he and I
had a heated argument

about our relationship
not being a competition.

I said, *I am who I am.
I can't be like*

*any of your friends'
boyfriends because*

we're all very different people
And I told him

he's not my whole world
because he can't be.

I said, *I can't give
anymore of myself*

to you, I said, *I'm all out
of pieces of myself to give.*

*But I do love you
more than I've ever*

*loved
anyone else*

in this way. I said,
Whether or not

*that's enough
is for you to decide.*

Communion

I was sitting on the floor
at the foot of his bed.

B. sat facing me
eye to eye

with his legs wrapped around
my waist like a hug.

I told my grandma
about me and you

last night while we
were folding quilts,

he said. All she said was
as long as I'm with a man

I can't take Communion
from the Church. She said,

Taking Communion
from the Church

is one of the most
important things

you can do
in your life.

Self-Portrait as My Sister: 1

today
on my way

to work
I saw

a woman
standing

in the middle lane
of I-70

crying out
for help

for her husband
who'd been

thrown
from his motorcycle

the paramedics
said we did

what was needed
until they got there

I can't get
the image

out of my head
of her face

as his hands
got cold

and his eyelids
turned blue

From A Letter

I've been on a few dates
since the break-up

with my boyfriend
who's Bangladeshi

and had to take a wife
he's his parents' only son

and doesn't want
to disappoint them

I understand but not really
anyway we've stayed friends

all that to say
I'm still learning

how to be in love with life
down here in Singapore

From A Telephone Conversation with My Mother: 2

Me: Sometimes I wish I was ten people
My Mom: Then you'd wish you were twelve

Telephone

in the end
he and i communicated
through her

she would say
he told me to give you his number
and for you to call him tomorrow

and i did and he didn't
pick up the phone

then she would say
he said he'll call you tomorrow

and he didn't so i called him
and he didn't pick up the phone

this went on for weeks
and weeks and weeks

i called him again on my birthday
just to try'n say hi
and was sent straight to voicemail

when i hung up
my first thought was

what if he's already gone

Love: 2

she said
love is

a lot like
a shadow

chase it
and it runs away

stand still
and it will

always
be with you

Transcendence

after the lungs
have breathed

their last breath
and the heart

has stopped
there's an energy

that won't allow
the body to slack

until its aura
has left the room

for my grandpa
it took two hours

that's what writing
is like for me

by the time
I finish a poem

being alive
makes sense

Sergio: 2

Today, the video documenting the incident that killed my cousin, Sergio, last year was released.

Today, I decided to let go of the anger at people I've been angry at for a long time.

One, I even tried my hand at resolution with. And since gossip ruins worlds, I asked what her problem with was.

She said it didn't matter then walked away.

Trying To Pay Bills

I was living downtown
working my ass off at Tennyson Center
trying to pay bills
I was only making
eleven dollars an hour
and there was this lady
holding a sign on the corner
outside my apartment building
saying she was pregnant
one morning on my way to work
I rolled my window down and told'er
you've been holding that sign
for a year-and-a-half
she said she'd lost the baby
I never saw her again
I hope she didn't kill herself

Going to Bed

B. was already asleep
in bed when I slid

under the covers
then scooched my body

close to his
so his butt was in my lap

as I draped my right arm
over his middle

he pulled my hand
onto his stomach

so my palm lay flat
across his bellybutton

he held his hand
on top of mine

and squeezed it
like a squeegee

I smiled and kissed him
on the back of his neck

then closed my eyes
and went to sleep

Something New and Gentle

my mom my brother and I
met my brother-in-law's parents

in the doctor's office waiting room
where the five of us anxiously chattered

about whether or not we wanted
the baby to be a boy or a girl

until my brother-in-law appeared
a half-a-hour later

and led us down the hall
to an exam room with closed door

the other side of which my sister lay
shiny baby bump up and jellied

while the ultrasound technician
explained the sonogram image

of a healthy cucumber squash-sized fetus
floating in amniotic ocean

my mom knocked and asked
if we could all come in all at once

my sister said *yes yes yes*
come in please come in

Self-Portrait as My Sister: 2

I was at work yesterday
When a guy walks in

With ice cycles dangling
From his clothes and beard

"I've already been treated
For really bad frost bite,"

He says, "Everything hurts.
I am struggling to walk

"I'm looking
For the shelter."

*Unfortunately, we don't have
Open beds available to the public*

*Here in the hospital, I say,
But let's get you a dry blanket,*

*Then see if we can
Get you some help.*

And of course we did.
Luckily, he was only

Two blocks away from a shelter.
They take walk-ins till 7.

"What time is it, please?" he asks
It's 6: 25. You still have time.

He says "Thanks" then walks back out
Into the cold three degree night.

On Kit's First Birthday Since Her Death

Kit, happy birthday.
It's your birthday, Kit.

Thank you for being my friend
And for helping me understand

What being a friend means.
Thanks for letting me

Hold your hand and cry
the night before you died.

I miss you and love you
And am happy for you.

Thank you for letting me take you
On doctors appointments.

Thank you for letting me
Help take care of you

When you were sick.
Thank you for teaching me

That some goodbyes
Take a long time. Thank you.

Thank you. Thank you.
Thank you. Thank you.

Also, happy birthday
Beautiful lady. Goodbye.

Pregnancy

my breast are burning
like drought fed fire

my nipples are peeling
like old wall-paint chips

my acupuncturist
prescribed barley sprout

I've cried midnight tears
and tried cool rags and cream

nothing soothes the pain
of being a world

Buddhahood

the viewing
of my cousin's

body was yesterday
at the mortuary

a clean
single shot

to the left side
of his head

which is strange
because he was

right handed
and only twenty-nine

I once heard it said
that suffering

is the pain
of staying the same

being greater
than the pain

of making
a change

today
we bury him

www.ingramcontent.com/pod-product-compliance
Lightning Source LLC
Chambersburg PA
CBHW032126090426
42743CB00007B/483